TONE AND TECHNIQUE

THROUGH CHORALES AND ETUDES

BY JAMES D. PLOYHAR AND GEORGE B. ZEPP

D1408388

AN IDEAL COMBINATION
FOR THE IMPROVEMENT OF TECHNICAL FACILITY,
ARTICULATION, INTONATION AND TONE

FOREWORD

This unusual book brings to music educators and students of today some of the time-honored studies by Arban, Klose, Concone, Shantl, Pares and Saint-Jacome. They are presented in an interesting format with twenty-four of the most popular chorales from traditional literature.

THE CHORALES

To insure a rich, full band sound all chorales are scored in four basic parts (A-B-C-D). They may also be performed very effectively by any small ensemble in which all four parts are represented. Some of the more obvious of many possible instrumental combinations are:

BRASS QUARTET: 1st Trumpet (A) 2nd Trumpet (B) 1st Trombone or Horn
                      (C) 2nd Trombone or Horn (D)
CLARINET QUARTET: 1st Clarinet (A) 2nd Clarinet (B) Alto Clarinet (C) Bass Clarinet (D)
SAXOPHONE QUARTET: 1st Alto (A) 2nd Alto (B) Tenor (C) Baritone (D)

THE ETUDES

These excellent studies can be played in unison by the entire band or band class. The director may then assign the etude to any section or combination of instruments, while the remainder of the group plays the BAND PART. Like the chorales, these accompaniments are scored in four basic parts (A-B-C-D). Harmonically and rhythmically complete, they transform the useful "exercise" into an enjoyable musical experience.

THE DUETS

Written by acknowledged masters of instrumental pedagogy, the six duets add yet another dimension to musical growth and development. The band is divided into two balanced sections in any manner the director may choose. The two parts are written to provide equal challenge for all players. Repetition without monotony may be achieved by exchanging parts for a second playing.

SPECIALIZED SCALE AND TECHNICAL STUDIES

The final section consists of etudes composed for particular families of instruments by specialists in each category. The SIX SCALE STUDIES for woodwind instruments are by Pares, with brass accompaniments by James D. Ployhar. The EIGHT TECHNICAL STUDIES, written for brass instruments by Arban and Saint-Jacome, have woodwind accompaniment. All of these etudes offer valuable and challenging technical workouts designed to meet specific needs.

INSTRUMENTATION AND PART ASSIGNMENT

Conductor	Bb Bass Clarinet (D)	Eb Baritone Saxophone (D)	Baritone T.C. (D)
Flute (A-8va higher)	Oboe (A)	Bb Trumpet/Cornet (A-B)	Baritone B.C. (D)
Eb Clarinet (A)	Bassoon (D)	Horn in F (C)	Bass (Tuba) (D-8va lower)
Bb Clarinet (A-B)	Eb Alto Saxophone (A-B)	Horn in Eb (Mellophone) (C)	Drums (rhythm)
Eb Alto Clarinet (C)	Bb Tenor Saxophone (C)	Trombone (C-D)	Bells (A)

CONTENTS

CHORALES

Student Book

O THOU JOYFUL DAY - Sicilian Folk Song 3
SEE, THE CONQUEROR MOUNTS IN TRIUMPH - Dutch Trad. Melody 4
YE WATCHERS AND YE HOLY ONES - German Traditional 5
HYMN TO JOY - Ludwig van Beethoven 6
THE GOD OF ABRAHAM PRAISE - Traditional Hebrew Melody 7
O WORD OF GOD INCARNATE - German Chorale 8
O WORSHIP THE KING - Michael Haydn 9
EIN'FESTE BURG - Martin Luther 10
SLEEPERS, WAKE - J. S. Bach 11
AGAIN, AS EVENING'S SHADOW FALLS 12
WITH SONGS AND HONORS SOUNDING LOUD - Trad. German Melody 13
COME, CHILDREN, JOIN TO SING - Spanish Melody 14
GOOD MEN, REJOICE - German Medieval Melody 15
INTEGER VITAE - Friedrich F. Fleming 16
COME, MY SOUL, THOU MUST BE WAKING - Franz Josef Haydn 17
AUSTRIAN CHORALE - Franz Josef Haydn 18
NOW THANK WE ALL OUR GOD - Johann Cruger 19
LO, HOW A ROSE - 16th Century Melody 20
VESPER CHORALE - D. Bortniansky 21
GREENLAND - Michael Haydn 22
GREENSLEEVES - Old English Melody 23
FATHER, BLESSING EVERY SEEDTIME - Sir Arthur S. Sullivan 24
BREAK FORTH, O BEATEOUS HEAVENLY LIGHT - J. S. Bach 25
CREATION - Franz Josef Haydn 26

ETUDES

1. FOUR EIGHT NOTES IN CONTRAST TO HALF NOTES - Klose 3
2. STACCATO EIGHTH NOTES - Klose 4
3. EIGHTH AND SIXTEENTH NOTES - Klose 5
4. EIGHTH NOTE FOLLOWED BY TWO SIXTEENTH NOTES - Arban 6
5. DOTTED EIGHTHS AND SIXTEENTHS - Arban 7
6. DOTTED EIGHTS AND SIXTEENTH IN $\frac{3}{4}$ HALF NOTES - Klose 8
7. MIXED NOTATION IN COMMON TIME - Concone 9
8. ALLA BREVE or CUT TIME - Klose 10
9. SYNCOPATION AND TIES FROM BAR TO BAR - Klose 11
10. TRIPLETS 12
11. TRIPLETS ON THE FIRST QUARTER NOTE - Klose 13
12. STUDY IN $\frac{3}{8}$ TIME 14
13. SLOW $\frac{6}{8}$ TIME - Arban 15
14. FAST $\frac{6}{8}$ TIME 16
15. VARIATION ON A FAMOUS MELODY - Arban 17
16. STUDY IN $\frac{9}{8}$ TIME 18
17. MIXED NOTATION IN $\frac{9}{8}$ Time - Schantl 19
18. STUDY IN $\frac{12}{8}$ TIME - Arban 20

DUETS

19. DUET IN ALLA BREVE or CUT TIME - Saint-Jacome 21
20. DUET IN FAST $\frac{6}{8}$ TIME - Tollot 22
21. STACCATO EIGHTH NOTES and SNYCOPATION - Saint-Jacome 23
22. MIXED NOTATION IN $\frac{2}{4}$ - Saint-Jacome 24
23. MIXED NOTATION IN ALLA BREVE or CUT TIME - Saint-Jacome 25
24. DUET IN SLOW $\frac{6}{8}$ TIME - Saint-Jacome 26

WOODWIND SCALE STUDIES WITH BRASS ACCOMPANIMENT

25. SCALE STUDY IN Bb (Concert) - Pares 27
26. SCALE STUDY IN Eb (Concert) - Pares 27
27. SCALE STUDY IN C (Concert) - Pares 28
28. SCALE STUDY IN F (Concert) - Pares 28
29. SCALE STUDY IN Db (Concert) - Pares 29
30. SCALE STUDY IN Ab (Concert) - Pares 29

TECHNICAL STUDIES FOR BRASS INSTRUMENTS WITH WOODWIND ACCOMPANIMENT

31. VELOCITY STUDY WITH EIGHTH NOTES - Arban 30
32. VELOCITY STUDY WITH TRIPLETS - Saint-Jacome 30
33. INTERVAL STUDY - Saint-Jacome 31
34. VELOCITY STUDY WITH SIXTEENTH NOTES - Saint-Jacome 31
35. DOUBLE TONGUING - Arban 32
36. DOUBLE TONGUING - Arban 32
37. TRIPLE TONGUING - Arban 32
38. TRIPLE TONGUING - Saint-Jacome 32

O Thou Joyful Day

Sicilian Folk Song

Four Eighth Notes in Contrast to Half Notes

Etude No. 1

Klose

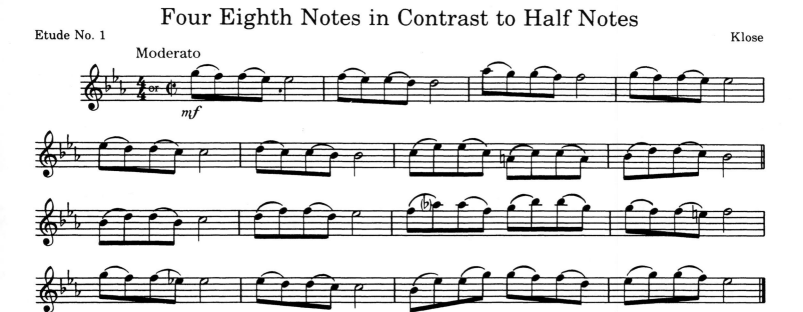

Band Part

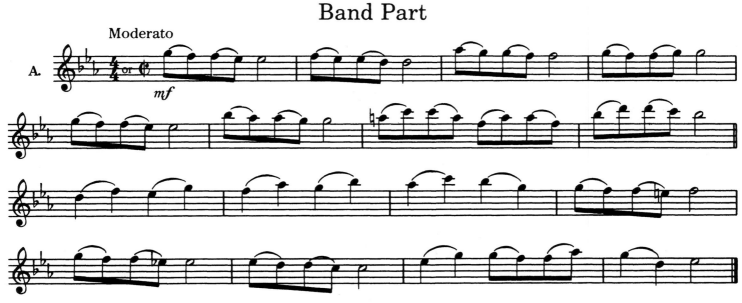

E.L. 3174

See, the Conqueror Mounts in Triumph

Dutch Traditional Melody

A.

Staccato Eighth Notes

Etude No. 2

Klose

Moderato

mf

Fine

D. C. al Fine

Band Part

Moderato

A.

mp

Fine

D. C. al Fine

Ye Watchers and Ye Holy Ones

German Traditional

Eighth and Sixteenth Notes

Etude No. 3

Klose

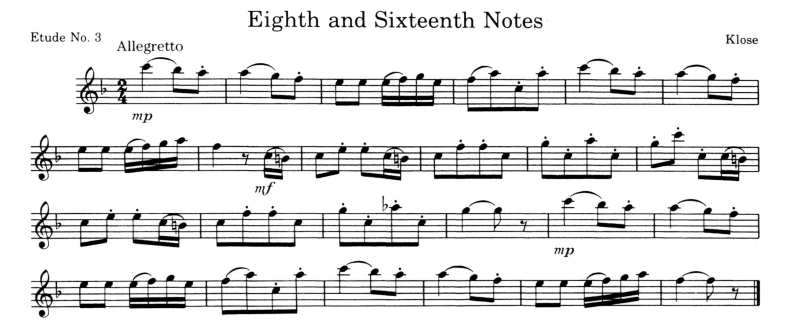

Band Part

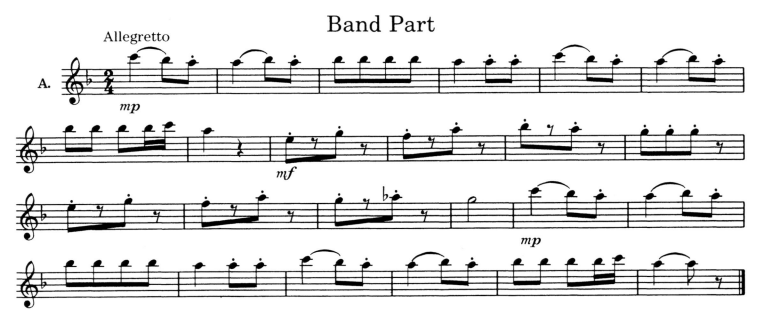

Hymn to Joy

Ludwig van Beethoven

A.

Eighth Notes Followed by Two Sixteenth Notes

Etude No. 4

Arban

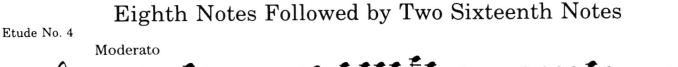

Moderato

mf

Band Part

Moderato

A.

mp

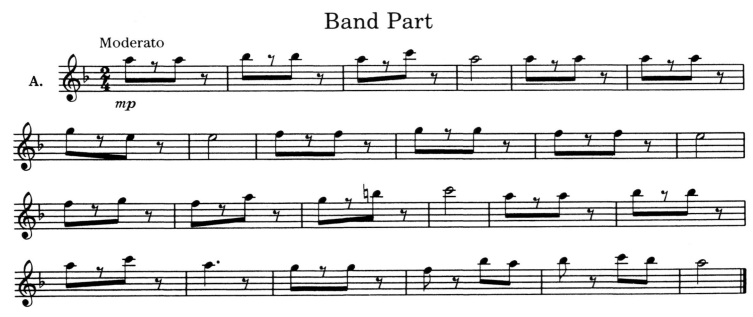

The God of Abraham Praise

Traditional Hebrew Melody

Dotted Eighths and Sixteenths

Etude No. 5

Arban

Band Part

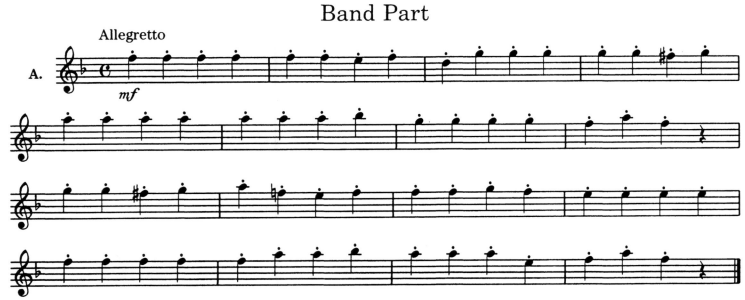

O Word of God Incarnate

German Chorale

A.

Dotted Eighths and Sixteenths in 3/4

Etude No. 6

Klose

Moderato

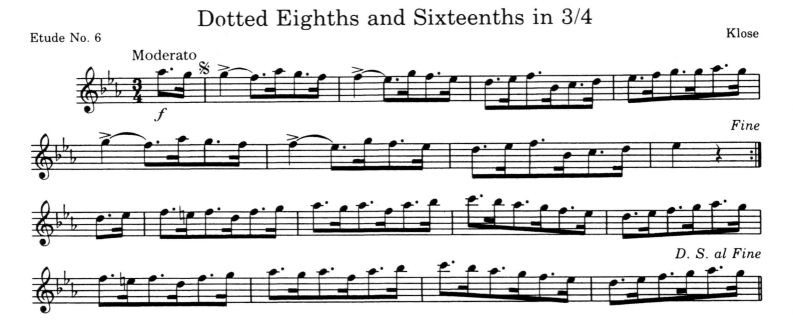

Band Part

Moderato

A.

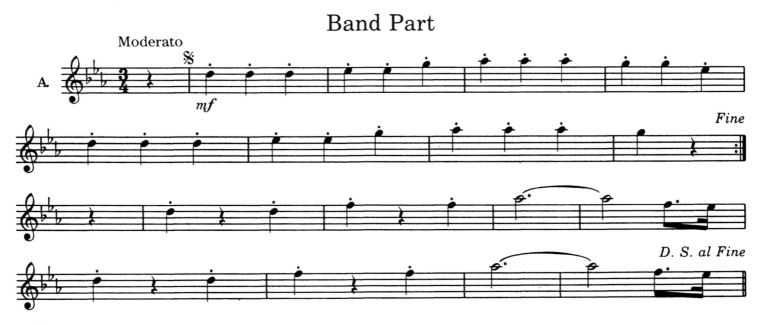

O Worship the King

Michael Hadyn

Mixed Notation in Common Time

Etude No. 7   Allegro

Concone

Band Part

Allegro

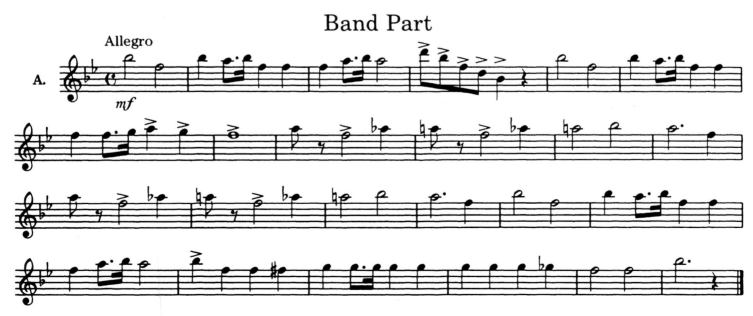

E.L. 3174

Ein' Feste Burg

Luther

Alla Breve or Cut Time

Etude No. 8

Klose

Band Part

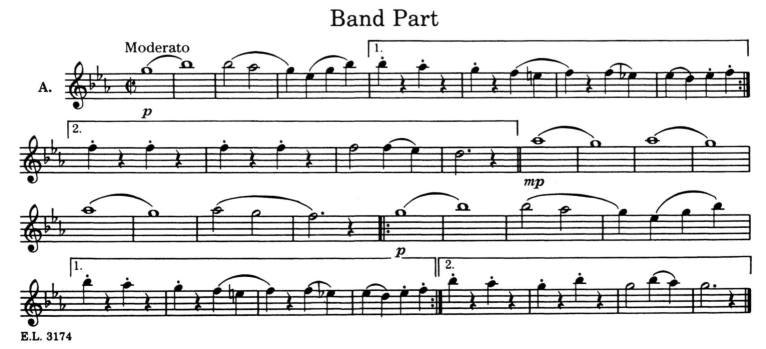

Sleepers, Wake

Johann Sebastian Bach

Syncopations and Ties from Bar to Bar

Etude No. 9

Klose

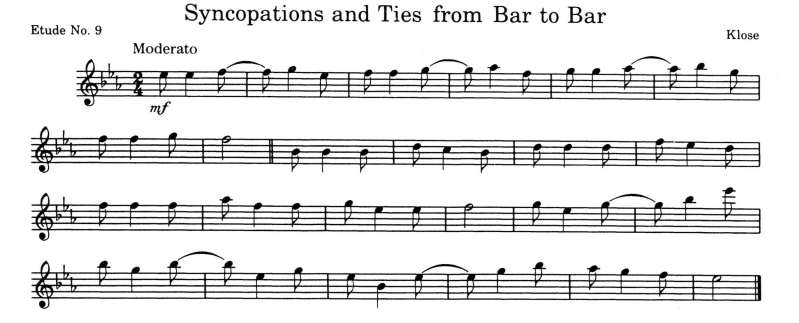

Band Part

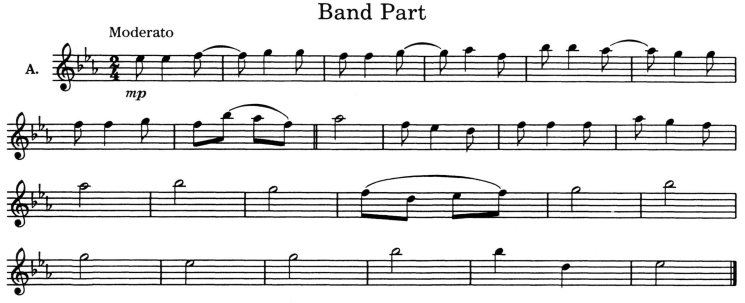

Again, as Evening's Shadow Falls

Jeremiah Clark

A.

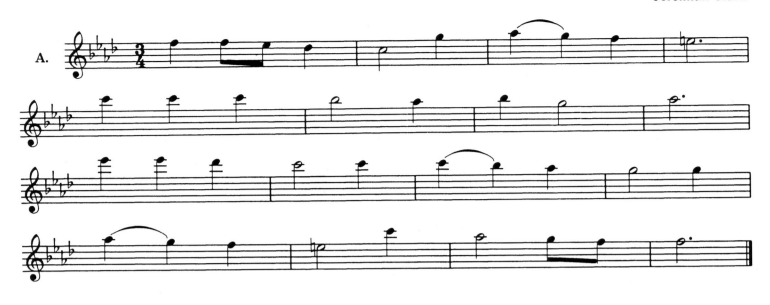

Triplets

Etude No. 10

Maestoso

Band Part

Maestoso

A.

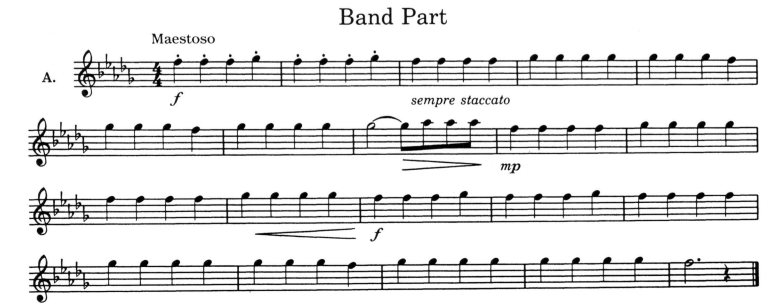

E.L. 3174

With Songs and Honors Sounding Loud

Traditional German Melody

rit.

Triplets on the First Quarter Note

Etude No. 11

Klose

Allegro moderato

Band Part

Allegro moderato

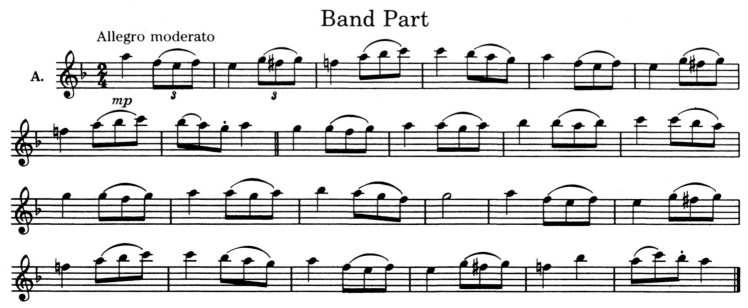

14

Come, Children, Join to Sing

Spanish Melody

A.

Study in 3/8 Time

Etude No. 12

Moderato

Band Part

Moderato

A.

Good Men, Rejoice

German Medieval Melody

Slow 6/8 Time

Etude No. 13

Arban

rall.

Band Part

rall.

Integer Vitae

Friedrich F. Fleming

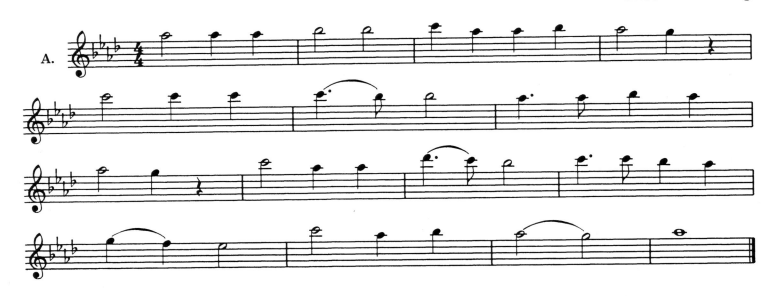

Fast 6/8 Time

Etude No. 14

Allegro moderato (In 2)

Band Part

Allegro moderato (In 2)

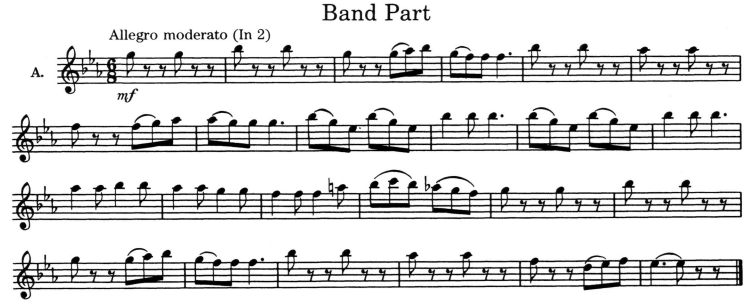

Come, My Soul, Thou Must Be Waking

Franz Josef Haydn

Variation on a Famous Melody

Etude No. 15

Arban

Moderato

Band Part

Moderato

E.L. 3174

Austrian Chorale

Franz Josef Haydn

A.

Study in 9/8 Time

Etude No. 16

Andante con moto (In 3)

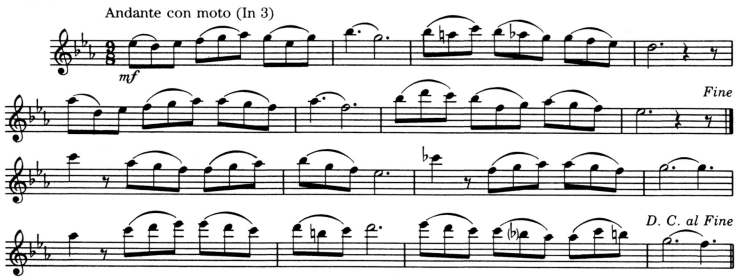

Band Part

Andante con moto (In 3)

A.

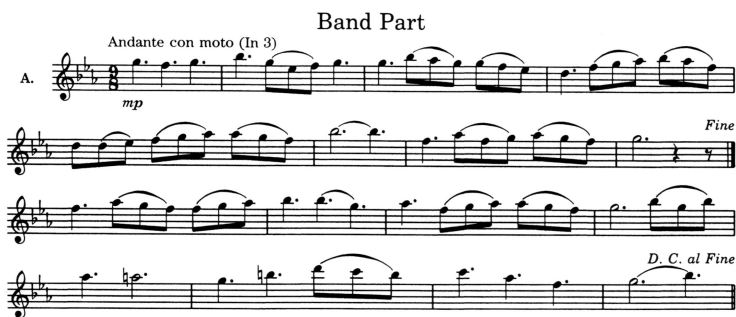

Now Thank We All Our God

Johann Cruger

rall.

Mixed Notation in 9/8 Time

Etude No. 17

Schantl

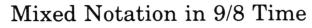

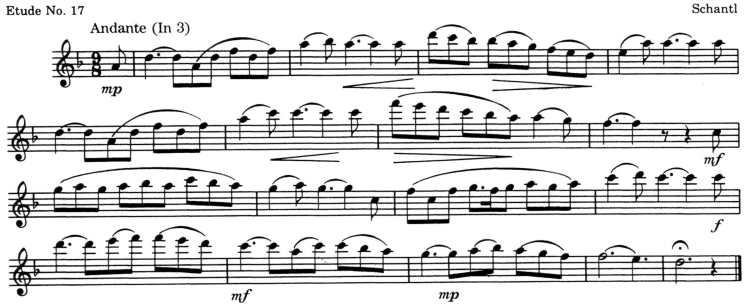

Band Part

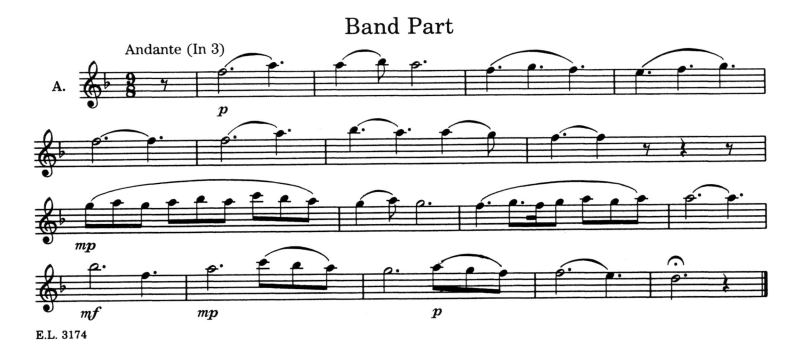

Lo, How a Rose

16th Century Melody

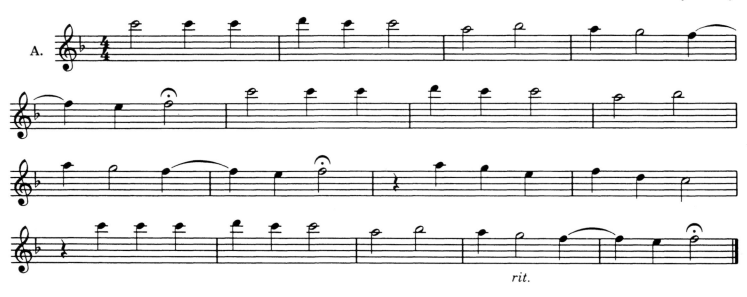

rit.

Study in 12/8 Time

Etude No. 18

Arban

Band Part

Vesper Chorale

Ascribed to
D. Bortnyanski

A.

Duet in Alla Breve or Cut Time

Etude No. 19

Saint-Jacome

Moderato

mf

p

f

Duet Part

Moderato

mf

p

f

Greenland

Michael Haydn

A.

rit.

Duet in Fast 6/8 Time

Etude No. 20

Tollot

Allegro moderato (In 2)

Duet Part

Allegro moderato (In 2)

Greensleeves

Old English Melody

A.

Staccato Eighth Notes and Syncopation

Etude No. 21 Allegretto

Saint-Jacome

Duet Part

Allegretto

Father, Blessing Every Seedtime

Sir Arthur S. Sullivan

Mixed Notation in 2/4

Etude No. 22

Saint-Jacome

Duet Part

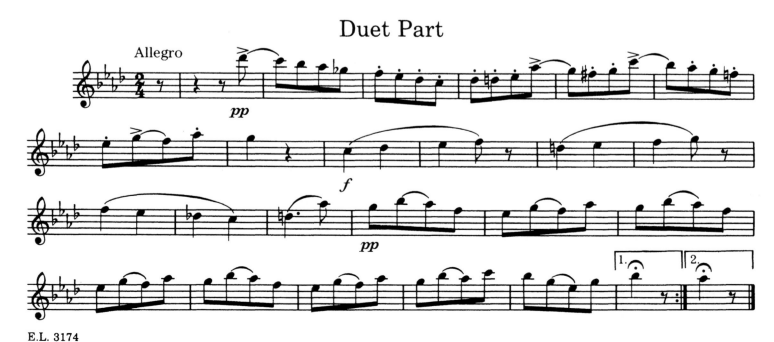

Break Forth, O Beauteous Heavenly Light

Johann Sebastian Bach

A.

Mixed Notation in Alla Breve or Cut Time

Etude No. 23

Saint-Jacome

Moderato

Duet Part

Moderato

Creation

Franz Josef Haydn

A.

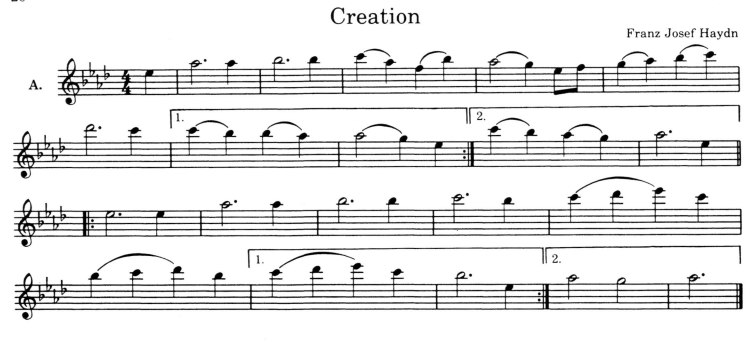

Duet in Slow 6/8 Time

Etude No. 24

Saint-Jacome

Andante (In 6)

mf

rit.

a tempo

Duet Part

Andante (In 6)

mf

a tempo

rit.

Scale Study in B♭ (Concert)

Etude No. 25

(Woodwinds Only)

Pares

Scale Study in E♭ (Concert)

(Woodwinds Only)

Etude No. 26

Pares

Scale Study in C (Concert)
(Woodwinds Only)

Etude No. 27

Pares

Scale Study in F (Concert)
(Woodwinds Only)

Etude No. 28

Pares

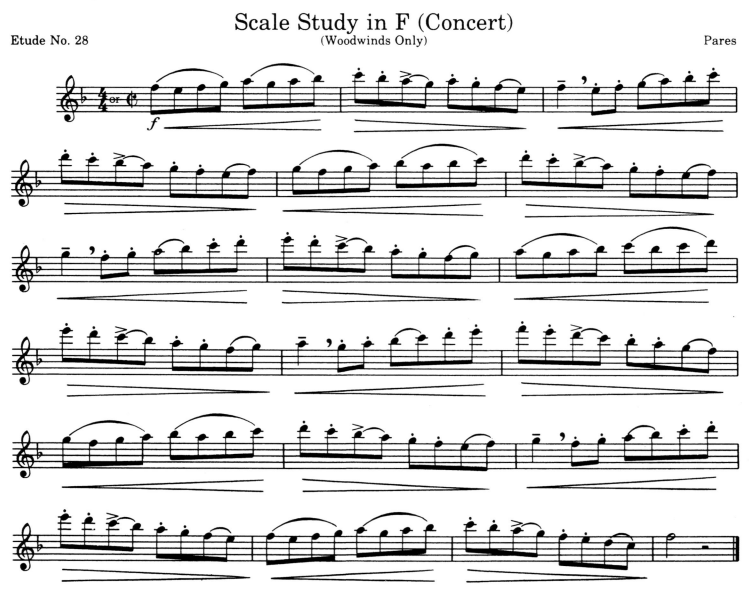

Scale Study in D♭ (Concert)
(Woodwinds Only)

Etude No. 29

Pares

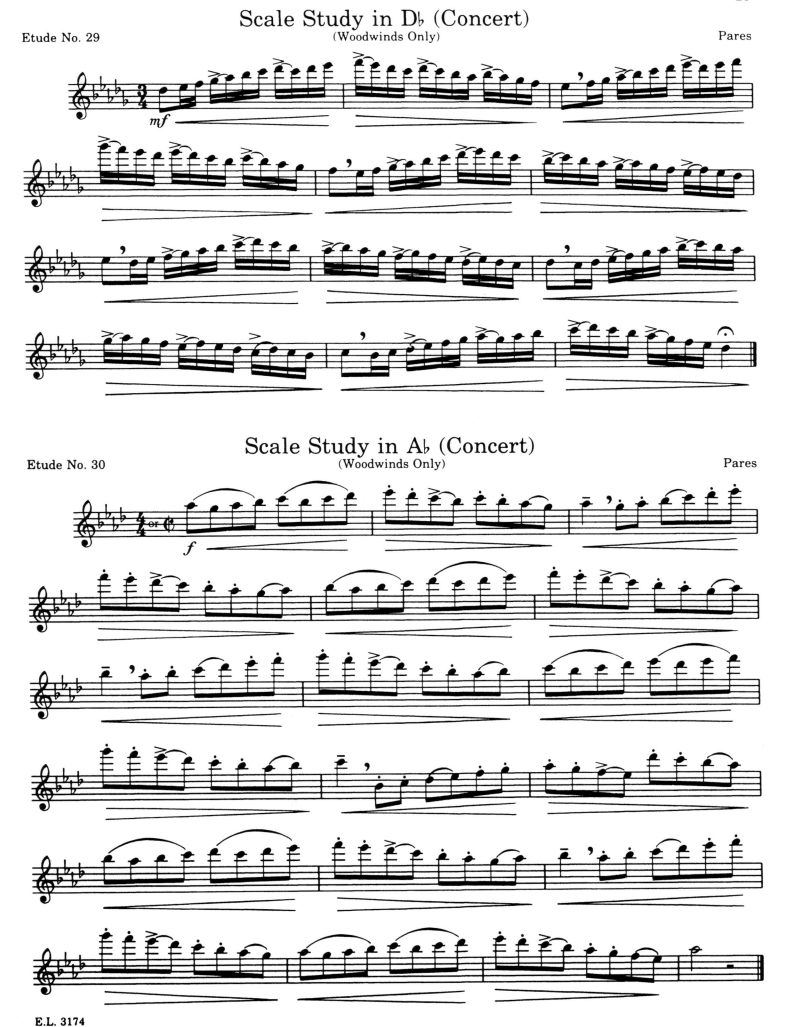

Scale Study in A♭ (Concert)
(Woodwinds Only)

Etude No. 30

Pares

Velocity Study with Eighth Notes

(Brasses Only)

Etude No. 31
(Band Accompaniment)

Arban

Velocity Study with Triplets

(Brasses Only)

Etude No. 32
(Band Accompaniment)

Saint-Jacome

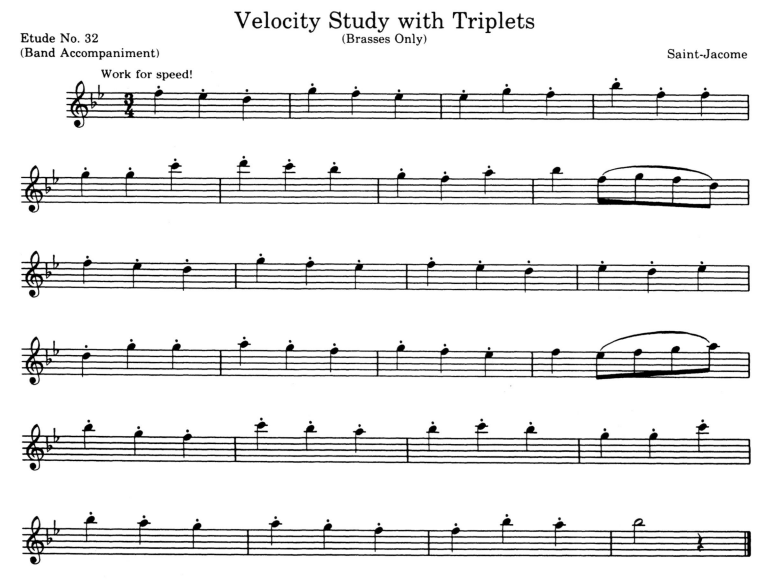

Interval Study
(Brasses Only)

Etude No. 33
(Band Accompaniment)

Saint-Jacome

Velocity Study with Sixteenth Notes
(Brasses Only)

Etude No. 34
(Band Accompaniment)

Saint-Jacome

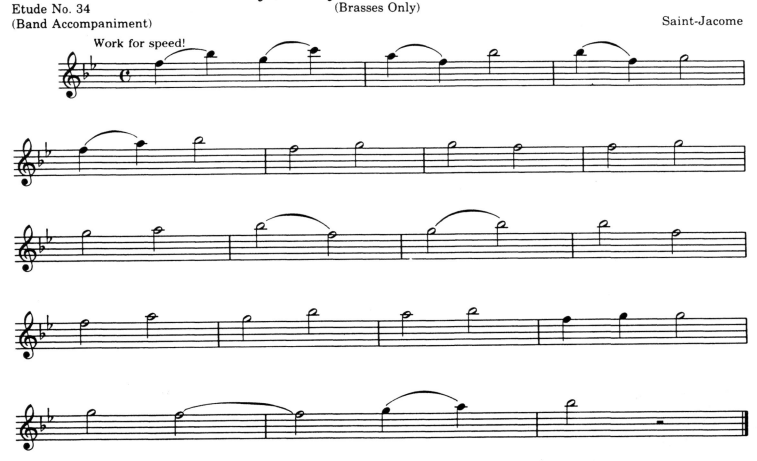

Double Tonguing
(Brasses Only)

Etude No. 35
(Band Accompaniment)

Arban

Double Tonguing
(Brasses Only)

Etude No. 36
(Band Accompaniment)

Arban

Various speeds

Triple Tonguing
(Brasses Only)

Etude No. 37
(Band Accompaniment)

Arban

sempre staccato

Triple Tonguing
(Brasses Only)

Etude No. 38
(Band Accompaniment)

Saint-Jacome

Various speeds

E.L. 3174